Leadership is Warfare: How to become the Modern Day Machiavelli and Sun Tzu and slaughter your competition in Business

I0492539

By Michael Schwartz

Table of Contents

INTRODUCTION

War- the necessary menace that we all hate to admit!

Since time immemorial, man has always been known to want the best for himself and the ones he cares about. Hence, in the distribution and struggle for (scarce) resources and because we all want the best for ourselves, we are more likely to have conflicting interests every now and then because there are about 7 billion people in the world and you expect egos not to clash? Hell will probably have to shed some ice before this happens. The chances that there are about 10,000 people that are on their way to a certain goal is pretty high and there is probably a higher chance that you would have to face certain competition on your way to achieving that goal. Since we all know that war is necessary (even though most of them are avoidable but for man's ego), it is best that we understand how exactly we can use war to our own advantage. No! War doesn't have to end up in a bloodbath or in a mass destruction of human life and property, war is the salt of the earth, who gets what and who doesn't is largely determined by war. There are several other people that want the same position that you want to get to in your workplace or in life and there is a probability that they are equally or even more qualified than you are. Since we have recognized that war is a regular and very normal occurrence in life, how then can you navigate through similar situations that have become necessary in the regular pursuit of individual and collective goals? You can successfully pull through by gaining a perfect understanding about war and how it works. That is what this book is about.

Competition is the salt of life and anyone that is going somewhere in life will understand the importance of having and overcoming competition wherever you find it. The people at the top did not fall there; they had to climb. No matter how good you claim to be, there will always be people that will want to oppose you. It is not always personal, most times it never is, it is just how life is and you have two options; you can choose to complain bitterly and get nothing done or you can enter the waves and find a way to stay afloat because there is a lot to be seen above 'sea level'. Take a look at every great person in history and tell me if they had opposition or not. We will all have to go through opposition or competition as some will like to call it. The struggle is constant if you wish to do anything meaningful in life; the difference between the successful ones and the ones that fail is how well they can fight the war that they are constantly faced with. No one really cares about your competition and how tough it is, as a matter of fact; the most coveted positions in the world can never be gotten to unless you are ready to step on toes and go to war when necessary.

In this book, I will love to highlight and show you practical steps that can be taken if you want to get to the top of your field. As much as it seems like a tough climb (it probably is), it is something that you are definitely capable of attaining if you put your heart and might to it. I would not attempt to sugarcoat my words and tell you that it is easy because in all honesty, it is totally uneasy to get great things done. On the other hand, it is not something that only a special breed of people can attain; the people that you and I look up to are just like you in terms of their physiological composition. What sets them aside from the rest of the crowd is the fact that they have come to understand that life is a battlefield and subsequently treat it as such. I like to tell people that they are the captains of their own ship. Whatever power or force you have decided to believe in, you believe in it because you allowed yourself to. Permit me to tell you that you can be your own greatest asset and you can also be your own greatest enemy if you do not do what you ought to. Get up today and make the decision that you will take life's challenges head-on and that you will be responsible for your own life and you will fight your own battles. The good thing about warfare is that you can never really lose; you either win or learn a lesson. If you lose a battle, you should never resign to that loss and begin to see yourself as a loser because that will only put you in more misery. What do you do when you lose a war? Find out what gave you out to your enemy, reorganize, plan and execute.

Lastly, you know how easy it is to tag some people as natural winners and others as being naturally unfortunate. Permit me to tell you that there is no such thing as a 'natural' winner or loser, there are several factors that determine whether you are a winner or not. I will patiently highlight them during the course of this book. There are a lot of amazing things to look forward to in this book and I am very confident that it will change your life for the best. If you happen to be one of the people that have been wrongly tagged as being mediocre or as being a regular loser then you need this book. I will not only share practical tips that will ensure that you get to the top as a leader but I will also share tips that will help you to stay on top. So if you are a student, a worker, an entrepreneur, a politician, a sportsperson or whatever you decide to dedicate your life to, this book is for you.

As I would always say, "the view from the top is always much nicer". In whatever you do, strive to get to the top because the top is where IT is at. Have a lovely read!

CHAPTER ONE: BUSINESS IS WAR

Understanding the concept of war in business

As you already know, the business world is just like the rest of all other human endeavors. It is sometimes more thrilling and more competitive than other pursuits because it is a battle that is fought from one generation to the other. The business world is so competitive not only because everyone wants to make more profit than the next guy but also because in the world of business monopoly is every person's dream. If for example, I am able to own 50% of a particular industry it is only a matter of time before I would want to own 75% or more. As you strive to own a high percentage in the industry, the smaller businesses are waiting in line like a pack of hungry cubs to take over from you at the slightest chance. As the leader of a business, you have to regularly look over your shoulder and it is vital to build and nurture a reliable team of players or warriors that you would take to war if the need arises. Once you are able to understand the importance of warring in the business world and also the reality that every day that you go to work, there are forces trying to bring you down then you will be fine.

Have you ever taken out time to imagine why everyone in the world cannot be at least comfortable or wondered why some are rich and others can barely afford a meal? Religion will tell you that some people have 'grace' while economics will probably attribute it to some forces of demand and supply. The reality is that it is possible that everyone lives a life of comfort but there are 2 reasons why this will never be the reality; Firstly, humans are typically greedy and secondly, because not everyone will be committed to the process of being successful. Why do you think certain businesses fail and some succeed? This is the case because the business world is a battlefield and it takes the mastery of certain principles of war in order to be able to successfully navigate through the perils of the business world (which could be deadly to say the least).

Strategic planning in business

In order to understand strategic planning in the simplest of terms, I will use an illustration to explain it. Every day when you get out of your home, it goes without saying that you definitely have some sort of plan for the day; groceries, business meetings, shopping, visiting friends and so on. A normal person will never set out their homes without a destination in mind. Likewise, in a business, there has to be a formalized roadmap that will define business as a whole. I always urge people to look at the kind of end they want for their business and work towards it. A strategic plan gives a detailed description of your business and the direction that you wish for the business to go. Strategic planning should not be confused with coordinating, forecasting or budgeting. A strategic plan gives your business a sense of purpose and priority for the long term and this helps you in coordinating the day-to-day activities of your business. In order for you to properly position your business in a chosen market, it is important to have a game plan that the management of the business uses to execute the business' activities. Great leaders of businesses have come to realize that no business is too small to have a strategic plan.

As everyone knows, you can only get results from the things that you decide to focus on. A strategic plan will help everyone on your team to have a common set of goals and this is the best way to attain team success. If you can get everyone on your team to believe in the set of goals that you have set for the business as though it was theirs then you will have a team of people who will go to any lengths to make the dreams of the business to come alive. With a strategic plan, you can be sure that everyone's energy will be directed towards the same thing and this will ensure success. A strategy plan will help you to explain to the world the value your business offers.

At this point it is important to clearly state that there is a difference between a business plan and a strategy plan. While there are templates for professional business plans, strategic planning is done by brainstorming and knowing your market well. By understanding your market, you are able to create a "wish list" for your business. While the business plan is written in order to identify models, missions and objectives of your business and to intimate the reader (who is most probably an investor) with various aspects of your business from staffing to the location of the business to marketing , financials and other factors that you will need to meet the business objectives. On the other hand, a strategy plan will identify the steps/ strategies that you will use to meet the objectives that are stated in your business plan. Strategy plans can be made for different aspects of your business and you can conduct an accountability check to make sure that the business is dealing based on the laid-out strategies for success.

I have said a whole lot about the importance of strategic planning in the business. Now let's look at 6 key elements of a strategic plan;

1) **VISION STATEMENT**- This simply talks about where you want to see your business in the future, the 'future' can be anytime from 3 to 5 to x years. A vision describes the main reason for everything

you do as a business unit. For example, your vision statement as a business owner could be something like "to train up lawyers in order for them to conquer their locality and subsequently the world". A vision statement will cover all that you do as a business and it can be said to be the essence of your business in the first place.

2) **MISSION STATEMENT**- While a mission statement talks about where you want your business to be in the future, a mission statement talks about the daily steps that you take in order to arrive at the desired 'future'. At Sony for instance, the mission statement is "to be a company that inspires and fulfills your curiosity. Groundbreaking new excitement and

entertainment in ways that only **Sony** can. Everything we do is to move you emotionally". This is what a mission statement should look like.

3) **CORE VALUES**- What are the beliefs and behaviors that your business will use as a guide in a bid to achieving the vision of your business. For your core values to work properly, it has to be the guiding map for the activities of every member of your team. This means that every member of the team must understand and abide by the core values of the business.

4) **GOALS AND OBJECTIVES**- What are the things that you set out to achieve as a business owner? What are the short-term or long-term goals that you wish for your

business? In strategic planning, your goals should be clearly stated. For example, the goal of a business could be 'to have 30% growth in the next 5 years'. The goal has to be clearly stated for the sake of accountability.

5) **ACTION PLAN**- Now that you recognize the goals and objectives of the business, it is important to draw up a plan that will help you achieve these goals (and even surpass them). No matter how great your objectives and goals seem, without a plan that will help you achieve these goals, they are nothing but mere goals.

6) **EVALUATING PROGRESS**- Every strategic plan should have a way of evaluating progress. It could be on a

quarterly, annual or bi-annual basis. Whatever time frame you choose to use, it is important to be accountable and to know how far your business has come and how far it still has to go as a business.

When you hear amazing success stories like that of Facebook CEO Mark Zuckerberg or Apple co-founder Late Steve Jobs you will notice some particular similarities, both started as a dream in a garage. It is true that the greatest business owners are people that are great leaders that are not only willing to dictate but are also willing to show members of their team how it is done. Whenever you see an organization that is thriving, there is a high chance that the reason behind the success of the organization is the fact that they have a successful leader on board. A great leader is a visionary that sees beyond what other people see, they see opportunities where others do not and they know when to seize these opportunities. The thing about great leaders is that they fail too, but they are ready to bounce back from failure all the time.

Leadership is not a small feat and being a great leader means bringing your 'A game' at every point in time because you do not know who is looking at you. As a leader, it is your duty to always look out for, inspire, care about and motivate your team members to be the best that they can be. Attributes of great leaders are virtually the same thing in every field in life from sports to business to lifestyle to politics to religion and all other facets of life. Below are attributes of what I refer to as the '21st century business leader;

ATTRIBUTES OF A GREAT LEADER

- Fearlessness is the first and probably one of the most important attributes that every great leader (in the business world) must possess. As a leader, you must be fearless; you should not fear failure, oppositions or anything at all. It is important to forge ahead without any form of fear because fear always has a crippling effect on people and as a leader that is the last thing you want to have.

- It goes without saying that as a leader, it is necessary to know how to manage yourself properly because one of the major roles of a leader is people management and to be able to adequately manage people you should be great with self-management. Remember that in order to properly manage a business, you must master the act of managing yourself.

- Another attribute of great leaders is that they do not just act, great leaders act strategically in order to arrive at certain results. Every action that is made by this kind of person is a part of the whole strategy. Want to be a great leader? Develop a strategy for everything that you do and follow it to the letter.

- In order to lead effectively, a leader must have great communication skills. This is greatly needed because the only way that the team members will stay connected to a leader is through effective communication on the part of such a leader.

- Accountability and responsibility are necessary ingredients in the making of a great leader. A leader should be able to account for and take responsibility for not just his action but also for the actions and inactions of the people who he is leading. This is why it is important to ensure that you keep everyone in your team in check.

- Leaders are visionaries, they do not make refer to the past or make plans for the resent alone. Great leaders always have a clear vision for the future.

- When things go south, there are two kinds of people; those that cower and then leaders. Being a leader means that you are able to manage any situation regardless of how complex or difficult it is. As a leader, it is your duty to stay calm in the midst of any storms because your calmness will radiate through the ranks of your team members that look up to you and this will result in more productivity for your team.

- For your whole team to continue to be creative, it is your duty as a leader to encourage and foster creativity and innovation in your team members. By doing this, you are training those under you to think on their own and not just be puppets.

- Team building is one of the most important attributes of great leaders. As a leader, you cannot work alone therefore, it is highly essential to build a team that you can work with. You are only as good as your team it therefore you ought to pay serious attention to the people on your team, promote teamwork and inspire your team members to be the best that they can be.

- One thing about the business world is that although there are trends that work for folks, it is important for you as a leader in the business world to be open minded and flexible. Most times, there are new ways to open old doors, all you have to do is to keep an open mind and soar!

- As a leader, the network of friends and acquaintances that you are able will determine how far you can go. Networking is very important because you never know the person that you can meet as a result of knowing a mutual friend of that person.

- One striking attribute of a leader is the fact that a leader never takes no for an answer. Persistence goes a long way in ensure success and it is only when you can determine not to give up that you will see very amazing results.

- As a leader you will need to develop a thick skin, this means that you do not easily get offended by small talk or by people that try to bring you down. You know what you desire for yourself and your team and it is important to develop a thick skin towards the things that you hear. It is not necessary to react to everything that you notice as a leader.

- The greats in every field of life all have one thing in common- excellence. As a leader, this should always be your watchword. It should become a habit for you and as it does, it will reflect on the members of your team and ultimately increase productivity and put you on top.

- According to the famous fictional character 'Scarface', you should never break your word for anything in the world. Integrity is a very attractive attribute in people and a lack of it can cause a lot of harm. It is important for you to keep your integrity because it helps you gain the trust of people and in order to go far in the business world you need to gain the trust of a lot of people. Firstly, you need to gain the trust of your team members and eventually the customers that believe in your services/products.

- To be a great leader to need to have passion for what you do, this is very important because on the rough days when there will be little to look forward to (there will be a lot of days like that), it is your passion- more than anything else- that will keep you going.

- What do Apple, Microsoft, Facebook and their likes have in common? They all came to the game with an innovative solution to a certain problem. As a leader, innovation is highly important because it is the factor that will set you and your team aside from the rest.

- Remember the saying about the patient dog? Patience is a virtue that great men possess and it always works for them. By being patient, you can attract a lot of good things to yourself and your business. In the business world, you cannot afford to be impatient because it will not work well for your business. Make all the necessary moves that you need to make and wait for the reward.

- Most times the difference between successful leaders and those that fail is that while the successful ones take steps decisively, those that fail are often times unsure about their steps. Decisiveness helps you to be confident about your actions regardless of the outcome. A decisive leader is one who decides a line of action, sticks by his/her decision and eventually accepts responsibility for the outcome (whether good or bad).

- Great leaders are not only great in themselves, they carry greatness and they are mostly willing to empower others. Anyone who is afraid of giving power to others is probably insecure and insecurity and great leadership cannot go hand in hand.

- In leading a team of people, it is important to maintain a positive outlook as it will reflect all over the behavior of your team. In life generally, a positive attitude will get you really far.

- Nothing good comes easy and the great leaders in the business world have come to realize that persistence is the key to the success of a business. As a leader, you must be willing to make attempts over and over again because sometimes success doesn't come cheap.

CHAPTER TWO: THE LAYING OF PLANS, CALCULATIONS AND ESTIMATIONS

In the business world, it is very important to make plans that will continually act as a blueprint for your business. Earlier I talked about the importance of having a strategy and how it matters to your business. You do not want to be left without a plan for your business as a business owner or as the leader of a team in whatever industry your business might be in. In order for a business to be successful in today's world of business marked by its unique features, it is very important that you have a blueprint that will act as a map towards the direction where the business is going.

As a popular saying goes "those who fail to plan already have a plan to fail". The truth is that there is hardly any business that became successful by luck, for a business to become "lucky" in the first place, and then such a business must have made necessary plans or taken necessary steps beforehand. Why is it important for you to lay plans for your business? Why is it important to have the future in sight and operate based on what you look forward to becoming? If you want your company to become a multi-million dollar or possibly a multi-billion dollar company then you must be willing to make plans to that effect. One thing I always love to tell business owners is that the period where it seems like a business is at the peak of its affairs is the period that such a business needs to work the hardest. You cannot get to the top of your market and choose to relax, that is basically what I call "business suicide". The business world is war, every single day when your business seems to experience growth, there is a very high possibility that a similar business is planning to take over from you. Therefore it is not enough for you to make plans on how to get to the top of the list in your market, it is more important that you plan on how to remain there.

When you take out time to properly plan your business, it is quite obvious. Not only does this increase productivity amongst the members of your team, it also boosts everyone's confidence and definitely impresses your clients. The success of a business just like having victory in the battlefield is as a result of proper planning.

No successful company becomes successful by accident; it is as a result of adequate planning. I am a huge sports fan and one thing that I have come to cherish about sports is the fact that it shows you the unparalleled importance of planning ahead. If you plan ahead, you will be able to predict the future and there is a huge chance that you will have the solution to any problems that will arise later on.

Stay prepared

In life, change is a constant thing and in the world of business, staying relevant is not as easy as it seems. Circumstances are bound to change and unforeseen events can change the fate of a business. I always emphasize the need to stay prepared for the worst case scenarios in business, although that advice may seem somewhat pessimistic but it is the reality that people face in the world of business. The truth of the matter is that no one can perfectly predict what will happen in the future, you can at best make informed predictions. In order for you not to be caught unawares, it is important for you to always stay prepared, stay ready so you do not have to get ready when the storm comes. While we cannot predict the future, we can decide to adequately plan and prepare for it. By staying prepared, you are more likely to have a better response when the storm comes because you have always stayed ready. How then can you stay prepared in the business world? As much as we desire control and predictability for our business, the sad reality is that uncertainty is a part of business. I love classic stories about war because they tell you how important it is to always prepare and make plans for the future. In the business world, several companies and businesses have lost their relevance within the twinkling of an eye. The fact remains that nothing is guaranteed and the relevance of your business tomorrow is not guaranteed. Therefore, the best decision that you can make is to ensure that you prepare yourself and your business for the future the best way possible.

Finding your enemies

One of the most difficult things to do (mostly for the people who are less observant) is to recognize an enemy. They are in every aspect of our lives and most times, they even disguise as our biggest fans because they would rather avoid suspicion. I said it earlier that the business world is a battlefield and this makes it necessary for you to; prepare adequately, recognize the enemy and finally Strike. In any war, you are bound to have allies as well as enemies therefore it is important that after you must have prepared adequately then you should recognize who your enemies are. Unlike in the world of everyday human interactions, enemies in the world of business aren't always as a result of personal differences or because they hate you. Most times enemies in the business word are just people that wish for their business to succeed (at the expense of yours). The earlier you fish these enemies out then the quicker you can set them aside and burn them. I always urge business owners and leaders to embrace the idea of having an enemy. Having an enemy means that there is someone who would rather have the great thing you desire for you and your business and most times this comes at your own expense. This mere fact should act as a motivating factor for you to get to the next level.

There are various kinds of enemies in the business world. There are certain enemies who disguise as friends and these are the worst types of enemies to deal with. They act friendly with you in order to earn your trust and once you let your guard down, they strike you badly. One way to avoid falling into this trap is by not trusting anyone because by putting your trust in people, you are slowly digging your own grave. What I have come to notice over time that most times the biggest enemies we face are not other people but internal enemies such as fear, impatience, greed, laziness amongst others. Earlier I listed patience as an attribute of great leaders, patience will help you to notice certain character in people and this will ultimately help you to find your enemies and that is one major aspect in dealing with them. Once you are able to recognize who you enemy is then you should take out time to observe such a person/groups of persons and figure out the behavior of such person/set of people because by doing that will be understand their weak points and that is how you will strike them down.

Importance of planning

Planning is one of the most important aspects of running a business; it could be a large company planning its expansion or a small ne trying to gain relevance in its industry. The size of a business does not matter when it comes to planning; it is something that every business that wants to be successful must do in order to attain that success that they desire. Often times, i love to cite the example of a person going on a holiday trip; for that kind of trip you are going to make certain arrangements as regards where you'd stay during the trip and so on(except you are one hell of an adventurous person). In the same vein, it is very important to plan in a business because not only does it give you a roadmap towards the end that you desire, it also makes the journey a lot more easier as you are bound to make certain preparations for the months and years ahead. For a small business owner, you might not really see the point of planning (especially if you are the only one in the business at that time). In order for you to be able to successfully set your business strategy, you are going to need a business plan. Every business that exists is there for a reason or a set of reasons, there are certain goals, certain yardsticks for success, and certain needs that the business looks to meet and so on. Therefore, setting off a business without adequate planning is like testing the depth of a water body with both feet (which you will agree that is not very wise to do).

There are several benefits that come from having a business plan and I will concisely mention a few of them;

- A business plan will give you an honest assessment of your business' strengths and weaknesses (through the SWOT analysis).

- A business plan also helps you to properly state and explaining the strategies that you want to use when it comes to marketing.

- Also, having a business plan can be helpful with regards to getting the real value of your business. The plan will help you to understand how much your business is worth.

- Investors always require a business plan before putting their resources into the business.

There are several other benefits of a business plan that I would rather not bore you with. The whole point of this is to understand that it is necessary to make plans for the future of the business. The economy is not always very predictable and it can always spring up surprises therefore I urge you to always make plans looking forward and ensure that you follow these plans to the letter for the success of your business.

CHAPTER THREE: WAGING WAR – THE CHALLENGE

The business world has never been this competitive, the competition is at an all-time high and it is getting tougher by the day as more people are entering and more businesses are competing to make the most profit. Regardless of the industry you might find yourself in any location, there is always someone that wants the same thing that you want too and there is always competition readily looking for ways to defeat you. The business world is never a safe haven, it is a war front and you have to either wage war or be defeated. War is not just a matter of strength, it is 40% strength and 60% strategy therefore it is not enough to just decide to go to war at every provocation. War is important if you intend to show supremacy but it is not always smart to go to war without necessarily evaluating the resources at your disposal. War is necessary; however, it is very important to ensure that you are not fighting a lengthy war that will leave you incapacitated at the end of it. Even though it is important to fight the battle for supremacy, timing is a very vital factor because if you do not factor in the time that you are supposed to fight you might end up losing the battle or winning with more than half of your soldiers gone. This sort of a 'victory' isn't a good one. In fact, I do not see it as victory at all. Therefore, it is very important that you know when you are supposed to wage war upon your enemies.

Know when to war

There are a lot of business lessons that can be learnt from real time warriors regarding the issue of timing. Knowing when to go on the offensive is almost as important as winning a battle itself. In the business world, excellence is not necessarily about getting involved and conquering in all possible battles. Before you go and make it seem like a case of contradiction, it actually isn't. Sometimes it is not always necessary to enter into a battle in order to show your supremacy to your enemy; in fact, it is always the sweetest type of victory when you do not have to go to war before being victorious. It always feels so good to know that you did not have to go to your arsenal in order to defeat a competitor. Not just because it earns you more respect, but also because by doing that you are given the power to be able to control that competitor and what better way to show your authority than to be able to control your opponent? Therefore, the importance of war selection should never be undermined, as it is more important than any other thing when you are in competition especially in the business world. What is the essence of fighting a war that you are sure that you will probably lose? It is better to avoid that type of battle and be seen as being weak than to enter that kind of battle and lose woefully. Losing a battle should never be an option because if you lose a battle there might never be a chance for total recovery apart from that fact, it is bound to have an adverse effect on your morale.

In the business world, people will challenge you, frustrate you and so on in order to get a response from you but it is important to note that it is not always necessary to settle your differences I business through fighting. Sometimes, challenges in the business world are supposed to make you a better person because competition puts you on your toes. Instead of entering into a war with the person/party, you can decide to channel that energy into making yourself and your company way better. Do not waste your precious energy trying to prove a point. You do not have to prove to anybody that you are a great warrior; it is always a sign of no self-esteem. As human beings, we tend to do better when there is a competition. It is however strange that a lot of people do not realize this fact and they begin to choose sides in a closely matched competition. The essence of this kind of competition is not because there is a need to find a winner and a loser but simply to make both parties better by putting them on their toes. It is sad that many people do not realize this and then they take sides and act as though one party hates/is in conflict with the other. When two closely matched parties are constantly put in competing positions it only helps to make them develop to the best of their ability. Take for example, the duo that the world of soccer has made to seem like bitter rivals/competitors over the years: Cristiano Ronaldo and Lionel Messi. Both are amazing footballers but often times they are made to seem like bitter rivals and this rivalry has caused both players to stay on top of the footballing world for over a decade as they have both strived to be as great that they can be in the field of play. Another example is that of Kobe Bryant and LeBron James who have always been compared and sides have always been taken. The competition between Apple Inc. and Samsung is another prime example in the business world; Pepsi and Coca-Cola are also great examples of how war can help both warring sides to get better.

So you see, competition does not necessarily have to be about annihilating the other party, it could sometimes serve as fuel to push you and your business forward. More importantly, you should always know when to enter into a war and when to totally avoid it and focus on developing your company.

Know yourself and also know your enemy

There is beauty in warfare and this beauty can be quickly turned into ugliness if you do not patiently follow the right steps to ensure victory especially in the business world. If you do not know yourself or your enemy then you are only putting yourself in great danger as it is not only necessary to know yourself but to know the people that you are at war with. In the business world, it is normal to go out of our way to paint a livid picture of our enemies by closely watching their recurring patterns and strategies. This is done in a bid to anticipate what their next move might be and once you are able to anticipate your opponent's next move then the battle is as good as being won already. It is important to know the vital parts of your opponent's business such as their marketing, content, branding and other vital aspects of their everyday activities as this will help you to have a proper evaluation of what they do and how they do it and also help you to know what the future looks like for them. Ultimately, knowing your enemy properly will help you plan better for a war (if it becomes necessary). If you know all these, you will be able to intercept your enemy and the best art of this kind of interception is that they will most probably not see it coming and that is the best way to nail your enemy- unawares.

'The art of war' has not only been touted as a manual for strategic thinking in real time warfare alone but the knowledge gotten from that great piece of ancient literature can be used in any sphere of life. One of the most important principles in the book is that you should know yourself, as it is very important to do that in order to be able to prepare adequately for any battle. Knowing yourself means that you understand your strength and weaknesses, you must be able to look at yourself and give an outsiders' evaluation of your business. By doing this, you are able to properly decipher the aspects that you need to work on, also when you know yourself you are able to understand how you should properly respond to certain things that come your way. The right reaction to certain actions can be the difference between winning and losing in the business world. The wrong reaction to your competitors move could be suicide, if you respond with war when you are just supposed to look away or you look away when you are supposed to fight, the outcome could be suicidal to you and your business. The game of chess is a perfect example of the importance of knowing yourself before making the decision to make certain moves; every move on the chessboard is determined firstly by the pieces that you have. The objective of victory remains unchanged but the way to victory can be changed from time to time therefore it is important to stay flexible.

In the quest for victory, the importance of recognizing your identity is highly important and it is not until you have to war that you need to know yourself. Constantly check yourself and your business to have a clear picture of who you really are from time to time. It is very important to check yourself from time to time because change is a constant and we as humans are bound to change therefore it is important to watch closely for any changes that might occur. In the pursuit of success, it is absolutely pivotal to know yourself because it determines the strategies you ought to adopt in order to get to your ultimate goal.

For you to experience excellence in the world of business it is important that you have a clear understanding of who your competitors are. The continued existence of your business can be determined by external factors such as your competitors. It is important to know your competitors in business like the back of your palm and if you are stuck up on the things that you need to know about them, I would give you a few;

- It is very important to know what your competitor's pricing is like, by doing this you are able to keep your own price within the range and compete with them on a fair ground.
- Another thing that you should know are the areas that serve as the strength of your

competition, what do customers like about their product or service? I stated earlier how you should avoid the strengths of your competitor and attack their weaknesses. Once you are able to find out what your competitors strengths are, you will ultimately thrive by avoiding it and attacking their weaknesses.

- It goes without saying that you should know the weaknesses of your competitors. Sometimes your competitor's weaknesses could show you areas that you need to focus your strength on. Finding out your competitors weaknesses will help you to nail them properly in the business warfare.

- Positioning matters a lot in business, how does competitors position themselves? When you know about the position of your opponent, it helps you to properly position yourself before launching an attack on them and in situations like this, victory is guaranteed. How do your competitors position themselves? Do they pay attention to a particular age group or class of people? What niche are they focused on? Knowing these simple facts can help you to properly evaluate your business to see what will work for you and also help you to evaluate what the best practices are.

- Lastly, it is important to know what kind of competitor they are; they could be direct competitors or indirect competitors. Direct competitors are the businesses that have the same kind of product or offer the same kind of service as you. For example, if you are into business consultancy then other business consultants are your direct competitors. On the other hand, indirect competitors are those that do not necessarily offer the same service but meet the same need in an alternative way. Knowing the kind of competition that they are will immensely help you to identify the most effective marketing strategies to use against them.

Now that you know the importance of knowing yourself and your competitors, why don't you try it out and you would see the importance of knowing these facts. You probably already know yourself and if you don't you can take out sometime to rediscover yourself from time to time. It is important to constantly evaluate your business to find out about it, the fact that you did an internal check last year doesn't mean that you know your business this year. Things change from time to time therefore it is very important to constantly check. On the other hand, here are some helpful tips in understanding your competitors and using the information to your own advantage;

- **Shop your competition;** what better way is there to understand the way your competitors treat their customers than to get first-hand information regarding the way they treat their customers. Get someone that can be trustworthy and get to understand the way your competition treat their customers.

- **Talk to their customers;** it is not enough to act as a customer because that way you might not get sufficient information regarding their operations and what helps them to stand out from the rest. You can talk to some of their loyal customers. This is important because it will help in understanding what it is that has made those customers to stick with your competitors. By doing this, you could get some vital information that will help your business immensely.

- **Check your competitors' websites;** a website can serve as the window through which you can see the company from the outsider's view and by checking your competitors' website, you are able to peruse through the length and breadth of your competitors' business. If you are able to do this take note of the vital details that you will get from the website then you can plan your strategy properly and bring them down if need be.

- **Attend a conference;** conferences are huge eye openers and if you plan on taking over in a particular industry then it is important that you attend conferences because they can help you to know the people in your industry better. By knowing these people, you are able to find out who your real competitors are and that way you can conquer them.

- **Hire your competition;** another way to get first-hand information about your competitors is to hire people from there. By doing this you can get direct information from former players who can give you useful information that will be of immense help to your business. It is very important to note that there might be legal consequences if this is done wrongly therefore it is important to consider the legal consequences before taking action. An advise from me; do not cut corners, this can be and should be done with means that are legal.

- **Become friends with them;** Keep your friends close and your enemies even closer. In order to get the best out of your enemy you can become friends with them and in doing this you can get vital pieces of information that will help you build your business. If you can carefully win the trust of your enemy by being their friend then you will easily learn a lot from/about them

Capturing your market without destroying it

I will begin this part of the book with a quote from Sun Tzu himself, he said and I quote *"Generally in war, the best policy is to take a state intact; to ruin it is inferior to this ... For to* win one hundred victories in one hundred battles is not the acme of skill. To subdue the enemy without fighting is the acme of skill." Before you go on to ask if this applies to the business world, the answer is a resounding yes! It is important to capture your market but more importantly, you should endeavor to capture such market without ruining it. Take for example, if two nations are fighting over a particular area and in the course of fighting over this land, the land itself is destroyed and becomes a shadow of what it used to be. You will agree that this makes the whole battle for the land a pointless one; this is why it is important to ensure that in trying to take the market, you do not make it into complete ruins.

In order to prosper, you must find ways to capture your market in a manner in which the industry remains healthy and intact after all is said and done. Most of the major companies in the world have managed to do this; they conquered a particular market and then went on to further expand upon that which they had already conquered. For a business to be said to be successful, it must have survived and prospered through times regardless of how small it began. Market dominance can mean a lot of things to different brands but the underlying factor is that the business continues to grow and thrive with whatever means necessary. The 70s and the 80s was a thriving time for Japanese companies as they began to conquer markets all over the Asian continent and overtime found their way into the European market and ultimately the US.

The airline industry is one that had been bedeviled by the ills of one or more companies trying to take over a market. Price-cutting was the means through which market dominance was sought but this however led to several mergers, bankruptcies and restructuring that eventually caused the industry more harm than good. There is a lesson or two to be learnt from this scenario and other similar ones when the market was destroyed in the process of trying to conquer it. Therefore, it is important that in the process of trying to take over a market, you do not end up destroying it.

CHAPTER FOUR: THE WAR WITHIN

Building your army of soldiers

A wise man once said that for the enemy outside to thrive, he/she needs the help of an enemy within, those were not the exact words but I expect that the message is clear enough. I have written a lot of things about how the business world is a war front and how it is ultimately important to fight the battle head-on. In order to be able to fight this war and be sure of winning you will have to do it with a reliable army of 'soldiers'. It is my belief that you are only as good as the team that you have behind you, no matter how great you think you are as an individual; if you do not have a good team to back you up then you will never really experience great success. Therefore, it is very important to patiently build your team because they will eventually become a part of the quest for victory.

There are certain steps that should be taken in the process of building a strong and closely-knit army that will conquer any opposition and battle. I will outline some of them;

> **VISION**; It has been said that a team without vision lacks purpose as they do not know where they are going and this kind of team will definitely not achieve much. Therefore, it is very important to ensure that the people on your team share the same vision with you because when there is a common vision or a common goal

then everyone on the team will go to any lengths to make sure that such vision is achieved. People who have a shared vision are willing to work together in ensuring that those visions become reality.

➢ **COMMITMENT**: In building a team, it is important that you find people who are committed to the process of attaining collective goals. If you have people who are not committed as members of your team, you will eventually get frustrated because they will definitely not put in as much efforts as other committed members of the team. Therefore, in selecting members of your team it is important that you choose members who are committed to the success of the team.

> **ACTION**: Vision and action go hand-in-hand, having a vision is never enough as it is very important to pursue the vision wholeheartedly in order to attain success; In building a team, you should ensure that you find doers and not only talkers.

> **COMMON GOALS**: The reason why a team can work together and attain success is because they have a common definition of what they call "success". In the process of

building a team, it is very important to ensure that you build it with people that share the same goals as you because this makes it easier and more fun to work. More importantly, you will be able to set definite goals and collectively achieve them without unnecessary stress.

➢ **TRUST**: This is one very important aspect of team building and it is probably the most important factor to consider in building a team. If you build a team with people that you trust, you will definitely reach your goals more easily because each member of the team will be confident and most times confidence is all that is needed to do great things in the world of business.

➤ **CELEBRATE**: Every once in a while, it is important to take a time-out from the stress involved in the process of reaching goals. It is essential to cool-off sometimes and celebrate little successes with your team members because that will build the team's bond and boost the team's morale to tackle bigger problems.

These steps are not only involved in building a team but are also significant in the growth of the team. If you are able to follow these steps in building your team, you will definitely have a great team that will take over the world.

How to handle people correctly

As a leader, you are in charge of handling other humans and in managing humans effectively, you will need to do some things. Below are some tips that will help you to manage the members of your team;

-    As a leader, it is important that you trust the people on your team. It is not enough for you to trust them as it is also very important for you to be trustworthy because the people on your team constantly look up to you for guidance therefore it is not enough for you to trust them, you should learn to be a trustworthy person too.

- A leader who learns to show appreciation for the great deeds and the not-so-great deeds of the members of his/her team will definitely help the team to attain more.

- In order to improve productivity among workers, it is important for a team leader to develop effective work relationship with and among team members. In addition, it is important to create a great personal relationship between team members too. By doing this, team members are able to communicate freely and interact better. Ultimately, this will improve productivity and trust among team members.

- A leader has the role of a father figure as he is supposed to encourage the members of his team. Encouragement can go a long way in boosting the morale of team members and ensuring that they work earnestly towards the collective goals of the pack.

- As a leader, you should never undermine the importance of celebrating success with your team members. Not only does this improve the level of closeness in the team but it also helps to motivate the team.

- It is also important to give credit to team members when due, even when they do not perform up to expectation, it is important to give CONSTRUCTIVE criticisms.

- As a leader, it is your duty to believe in the members of your team.

- As a leader, you should endeavor to listen to members of your team.

- As a leader, you should trust the members of your team

- As a leader, you should motivate them

- As a leader you should inspire loyalty and team spirit, without this, there will be a disconnection within the team and this will have an adverse effect on the outcome of the team's efforts

- As a leader, you should learn to communicate effectively with your team members. You should find a means of constant communication with them because it is necessary in building and sustaining a great team.

Develop your character as a leader

It is very important to develop your character as leader because there are people who look up to you for guidance, direction, motivation and a lot more. Therefore as a leader, you cannot choose to ignore this fact, as it should influence every decision that you make. Whenever you consider the fact that there are people who look up to you and learn from your every move then you will pay more attention to the things you do.

CHAPTER FIVE: POWER, ENERGY & DIRECTION

Getting power

Power, energy and direction are things I would not feel complete about touching on without firstly highlighting a real life example of how a young man rose to prominence from the ground up to the top. His story is however not as smooth as it would seem if you got an opportunity to meet him. Before we go on to talk about our guy, let us take a minute or two to talk about how power is important. I like to quote "Scarface" a whole lot and he famously said in the 1983 award winning movie 'Scarface' Al Pacino said "in this country, you first get the money then you get the power........". It goes without saying that money doesn't come close to being equal with power. Power is as a result of strategic planning and actualization of goals. Power is about how well you can position yourself and well you can network use the network of people you know to make your life better and help you fight your battles. You are only as strong as your allies are therefore it is important to have the powerful people sitting around your table. How do you get power? Money is not the right answer (although it sometimes could serve as a tool if it rests in the right hands). Powerful people understand that power isn't gotten so that you can rest on your oars, the more power you get; the more you wish to get.

Most people have the wrong conception that power can only be used for evil without necessarily considering that we all have power in relative 'quantities' and the people at the upper echelon are made to seem like evil-doers when in actuality they are just like you and I with more power. If you are stuck in a foreign town and you make your way around your contact list and find someone that you helped a while ago to house you then you just used the power that you have. Daily activities that we do not even pay attention to are all ways that we use the power within our reach. Since everyone is bound to use power at one point or the other for whatever reason then it is only right to get it in abundance so that you can advance the course of your life with the least volume of stress. Now that we have established that power, just like war are necessary ingredients in the pursuit of greatness in the business then we can procced to talk about the real life example of how an old friend was able to get power years ago.

So it was my sophomore year in college and I was beginning to settle into the whole system of schooling (I never really liked the whole idea of organized education although I enjoyed the social aspects of school). As you would expect, I slipped out of the classes that I didn't fancy and I attended classes that I liked without necessary bothering about what field it was. Whenever it was time for tests, I would be absent because I did not register for those other courses at the start of the semester. On the other hand, I enjoyed hanging out with friends a lot and we partied in our own way (we were always indoors because we detested being seen by the multitude). It was during these hangouts- as we loved to refer to them- that I met this guy who was entirely down to earth, he would eventually go on to be a great inspiration to thousands of people. We got talking and I found out that we had similar backgrounds except from the fact that he was from a more religious home and his parents never really let him out (except he was going for some church activity). Over the months, we got closer and this was when I learnt life-long lessons on how to intelligently seek power. One thing that you should never forget is that in the pursuit of power, you should never come across as being desperate because that could just lead to a premature end to the pursuit of real power.

Back to my story about Jake, although he had a little stature (he was about 5'7) he always hung around folks that were older and more mature. It was until much later that I realized that was his way of getting knowledge and getting certain relationships that will change his life for the better. Several people sold different things in school in order to get extra cash as money was just never enough in school (except you had really wealthy parents). Jake hung around the bad guys, good guys, geeks, drug dealers and literally every kind of person. This brings me to another point, in the pursuit of power you are going to have to look beyond certain character flaws or habits that the people that you seek to get familiar with in order to get a bite of the big apple. It is important that you do not try to judge people based on certain habits because at the end of the day we are all sinners. Why then should you judge another man for sinning differently? Jake kept hanging around these people so much and ordinarily I thought he was doing it just to feel cool until years later when I looked back at everything with a more mature outlook. Looking back, I realized that he hung around those people so much that he became like an errand boy and he was always contacted to get various things for various people. Jake slowly was becoming a salesman as he was always the one being called on to make various purchases and he got his 5% commission. This went on for so long that it became normal for people to call on him and ask him to buy them literally anything. He became so good that he could sell water to a well and he did it with so much ease. As time went on, he realized that he could start selling these things to the people that needed it as he had created a large scale of demand. He had a problem getting supply initially until he came up with a scheme to raise money from the same people that he had created a strong bond of trust. He began to get his goods by himself directly from the makers of the products. Jake did one better for himself as he **patiently** sought for a deal that ensured that he got at least a 30% profit margin. What made his case so unique was the fact that he was able to get this sort of profit margin while selling at the same price as his competitors. This was made possible by the fact that he was able to get a chain of supply at a cheaper rate to meet the vast demand for the products. In a matter of time, his popularity grew around campus; so much that he barely had time to attend to all his customers. All through his rise, he built a team that handled most of the process of getting the products and the packaging. All he had to do was to look for the demand and he'd supply, he slowly became the Jeff Bezos of my school as he sold literally everything that students and even professors needed. He was able to use his power to get people to sell their businesses to him and he took over about 40% of student businesses on campus. He got so huge that he had to get an extra room as his warehouse and it did not stop him from getting schoolwork done in the process.

Eventually he was able to build a conglomerate that went beyond the four walls of college. He went from being the 'little' guy that hung around the cool kids to becoming the guy that everyone wanted to hang around. He owns a multi-million dollar enterprise today that comprises of businesses ranging from sales to real estate to lifestyle to entertainment. How was he able to rise and seize the power the way he did? One answer; strategic positioning and planning, Jake always had a plan and he followed it to the letter even though it meant sleepless nights and a lot of sacrifice on his part, he did not mind because he had his goal in mind. Now he sits on top of the affairs of a fortune 500 company and people find it hard to believe that he started from literally being an errand boy that only got $5 commission for doing the dirty jobs that many of us would ordinarily have done. Jake was able to enter into the war of business with little resources but with a master plan. This is the story of Jake; from the floor of the dorm room to the top of a skyscraper.

The use of alliance and strategic control

Do you know the amazing thing about alliances? If done properly you would likely not know where the weak end is. An alliance is like having a group of players in a team, although there might be special people on the team that are stand-outs but at the end of the day they are all part of something bigger than one person. People that have the most power in the world today (especially in the business world) are all part of an alliance or another. Imagine being a formidable force on your own and then looking for other formidable forces to form a union of formidable forces that will be reckoned with. This is how power works and this is why the most powerful people want to be friends with people that are equally powerful and at times more powerful than they are. In battle, the ones that continually get victory are those that can use their power in conjunction with other powerful forces in order to become undefeatable. If you are familiar with the business world, you would notice that most successful businesses love to purchase or join forces with other successful businesses and add it to their conglomerate or become a team. In an alliance of businesses, the goal is to achieve certain objectives that are the same or quite similar for individual businesses. This is very important because it offers a lot of operational benefits and this serves as an added advantage for all the parties involved in such an alliance. It also comes with several economic benefits and it helps you compete on a larger scale because you can pool resources together to attain the important objectives.

There are different kinds of alliances based on different factors some of which include the time frame of the alliance and whether the alliance is going to be a temporary thing or if it would be permanent. Alliances like this are done on a contractual basis and each side of the table is supposed to sign a legal document to ensure that everyone is on the same page. Beyond the formalities, alliances are very good for businesses as long as they are strategic. Before entering into alliances, it is very important that you consult people in the right quarters as that will prevent you from making any mistakes that will cost you. At times, there are shady people who will lure you into alliances that will not totally favor you eventually and this can be avoided by patiently analyzing such an alliance before entering it.

If done properly, strategic alliances will not only help your business to experience growth and economies of scale but it will also help you to deal with enemies and have you well equipped to fight the battle in the business world.

Avoid your competitor's strength, and attack their weakness

This is one hell of a war technique and it has can be used to win any war without necessarily fighting or fighting vigorously. Sun Tzu, an ancient genius in the act of war once said, "An army may be likened to water, for just as flowing water avoids the heights and hastens to the lowlands, so an army avoids strength and strikes weakness". Many great leaders have mastered this approach in business as they endeavor to find the weakness of their competition and they capitalize on that and continually focus their attacks on that aspect of their competitor's business. This is how it is in a game of boxing (and a lot of other sports) where players tend to watch their opponents previous games and then after they discover their weak points, they ensure to practice those aspects that their opponent is deficient in and when it is time to strike they do that without mercy. Fundamentally, the major task that you need to go through is the recognition of your opponent's weak points and it takes patience and a whole lot of intelligence to correctly identify these weak points and even more patience to use it against such competitor. It is not enough to explore the weaknesses of your competitor, it is equally important to ensure that the tables aren't reversed and your competition uses your own weaknesses against you. This factor should be constantly evaluated in redefining the company's strategy. As we all know power is control, therefore it is ultimately important to control your competition and never let them control you.

After you must have mastered this act, it becomes easy for you to penetrate the market and control that market because you have managed to control your competition and this way you can go all the way up. After you must have your competition under control, it is your duty then to find loopholes in the market and fill them up. You can find a need that is not being (properly) met in your market and then ensure to satisfy this need so well that the consumers think of you whenever they have similar needs. If you are able to get the love of the consumers through amazing services then you continue to control that market.

Also, it is very important that you stay as private as you can in order to prevent that your competition is not able to learn so much about your business that he/ she can hurt you with in the future. You have to remain mysterious and your competition will be confused because they will not know your strengths or your weaknesses. It is better to make them perceive your strengths as weaknesses and vice-versa because by doing that you are able to continually control the market and your competitor will not come close to you. By confusing you opponents with both your strengths and weaknesses, you will be able to cause them to use their strengths to their disadvantage if they try to use it against what they wrongly perceive to be your own weaknesses.

CHAPTER SIX: DEALING WITH (DIRECT) CONFLICT

Conflict mostly occurs when two or more people have contradictory opinions, now imagine how often this happens to you and the people that are around you. Understanding the nature of conflicts is very vital in turning clashes or oppositions into well thought-out ideas and opportunities. Not all disagreements should lead into conflicts if you know how to handle them. Conflicts are bound to arise in situations that involve more than one person especially when it involves making very important decisions. They could arise from various differences in ideologies ranging from philosophical, ethical, religious, moral differences and so on. Conflicts can cause the demise of a business especially when the business is in the developmental phase. Conflicts are bound to happen, however the problem arises when conflicts aren't properly managed and made to lead to further compounded disagreements and then escalate beyond repair. As a leader it is your duty to know how to handle conflicts when they arise amongst members of your team or even between a member of your team and external influences like suppliers and so on. I would not waste your time by giving you tips and tricks on how to avoid conflicts because they cannot be totally avoided.

Since it is true that conflict is a necessary aspect in a business, it is your job as a leader to ensure that the damage caused by it is at the barest minimum. As a matter of fact there should be some sort of process in place that will handle conflicts and resolve them amicably. Here are some things that you should know about conflicts:

- It not always the manager's duty to fix conflicts, each member of the team should be well trained to ensure that they understand how to properly manage conflicts in order to prevent escalations that might later affect the business. Unless the conflict arises from behavioral or performance based shortcomings then you as a leader might not even notice. Conflict resolution is important in the business world because you have a lot of opponents in the outside that are waiting for you to fail and therefore it is unnecessary baggage when there is war within your camp.

- Conflict is not always negative and the earlier you acknowledge this fact, the easier it is to resolve conflicts when they arise. Problems or differences should never be masked because that will only make matters worse as they would become bigger problems and this could mean suicide for your business or your team.

- More often than not, the foundation or the problem that is the cause of the conflict isn't clear. Everyone might not see the problem involved in the conflict except the conflicting parties and this is why it is very important to find the problem first before deciding to solve such a conflict. Ordinarily, as a leader you could order both parties involved in the conflict to resolve it and they will act like it but until the problem is spelled out clearly and a solution is proffered, such a conflict might still linger.

- It is not always the case that conflicts are caused by difficult people, sometimes conflict arises from pressure, confusion and other factors. It is very important for you as a leader to ensure that everyone understands what they ought to do and try as much as possible to make the working environment more hospitable for the workers because that way likelihood of conflicts will be highly reduced.

Often times, people assume that there are winners and losers when it comes to conflicts and this cannot be further from the truth. Sometimes, conflicts arise from holding on to a position and refusing to let go of that belief in such a position. Sometimes it is pride that is at play when people conflict and there isn't necessarily a winner or loser. Have you taken out time to listen to various reasons why people have conflicts? You will definitely be amazed at how a voidable most of these instances are.

While the goal is to preserve or repair a working relationship, this isn't always possible with all conflicts and in some cases you might have to step in as the leader and handle such conflicts.

Now that you know these things about conflicts and how they arise, let's go and to talk about how to contain/control these conflicts in order to avoid unnecessary distractions in the workplace. Below are some helpful ways of resolving conflicts, you should share this with members of your team as most of these steps can be done by them (without your necessary intervention).

Mediation; this is the easiest and quickest way out of a conflict and this is about the first step that you should consider as a leader. It involves having a conversation with both parties and understanding the cause of such a conflict, once the cause has been ascertained then you should find an objective way to go about resolving it. As a leader, it is your duty to not pick sides and issue criticisms where it is due. Mediation should never be coerced because if it is then you might just end up missing the whole essence of the process.

Compromise; sometimes it is less important to be right and more important to just get things done, most times if we look inwards at the main reason behind many of the conflicts we face it is majorly because we fail to compromise. At times, it is just good to make compromises because it is not always about being right or doing it your way. An African adage says, "There are a numerous ways to arrive at the marketplace" what this simply means is that there are several ways with which we can do things. Therefore, in order to move forward in one accord, a person might have to make certain compromises.

Voting; I will advise you to use this method for conflicts that involve critical decisions that need to be made. In a case where there is a debate between two marketing experts for instance regarding what marketing methods to use, you can step in as a leader if you notice that things are getting out of hand. The best way to settle this kind of conflict without making one party look stupid is by making other members of the team to go through the democratic process of voting.

Discussion and Written Communication; most times, conflicts arise as a result of misunderstanding and/or lack of proper communication between the parties involved. In settling disputes, you can organize a discussion between both parties and this is where they calmly state their dissatisfaction and make their stand clear enough. At the end of the day you might end up realizing that the conflict started as a result of one person misunderstanding the other and discussing it could be the easy way out. Also, written communication can help in settling disputes as people tend to be more articulate. As the leader, you can make both conflicting parties write letters to each other stating what the problem is and you will be amazed at the results.

As I stated earlier, conflicts are not entirely bad, as a matter of fact, once a conflict is properly and quickly resolved it brings the conflicting parties closer than ever. Below are some of the benefits of promptly resolving conflicts in the workplace:

- it increases employee productivity
- it provides a greater sense of harmony in the workplace
- it prevents misunderstanding
- it improves communication
- it increases momentum
- it builds a tighter bond and increases mutual trust
- it resolves disputes and prevents escalation
- it reduces liability and costs
- it helps to reconcile differences

CHAPTER SEVEN: TACTICAL VARIATIONS IN WAR

In life, it is common for you to hear people say complain bitterly about change, most times we all hate when it happens and we are not ready for the impact. Most people tend to live their lives by being prepared (at least that's what they think) to take on whatever comes their way. In life, we are always trying to assume that things will go a number of ways, anything beyond those anticipated outcomes will definitely constitute a huge problem as it is often not what we have planned out. Personally, I think that although it is important to make plans, one should always remain flexible because change is a constant and it can happen both when we expect it and can also happen totally unexpectedly. In the business world as well as life, we hate it when change creeps in on us because it might be very costly and I mean thousands and in some cases millions of dollars. Therefore, I always suggest to folks in the business world to stay on their toes because you never know when another "great recession" or something not as severe will happen.

Understanding change as a continuum

In business, change can occur at any time and there are several factors that can cause change to occur. In business (just like in life), change forces us out of our comfort zones and creates effects that may be traumatizing to say the least. Change in itself is not always bad because there are people who thrive as a result of change- whether sudden or not. What matters more than the change that happens is our response to it, if you can accept change and adapt to it then you will enjoy the positive aspect of change.

Change can be defined as a transition from one state to another state (in a business environment), most times change comes as a result of the unprofitability of the current state or because of the availability of better options with which one can thrive with time. Most times, change is said to be difficult mainly because it forces people out of their comfort zones. One thing that people (mostly the lazy ones) fail to realize is that with change comes experience, if you are able to adapt to a particular change at a point in life then you have gained experience in handling such situations and in the future, when similar situations occur, you will be able to face such a situation head-on. If you can take positive steps when change comes and do your best to resist the hurdles that will definitely come your way then you will be better off for it.

About 65-70% of senior executives in large companies will answer a resounding yes to the question of whether they love stability in business. I wouldn't lie and say that I don't love stability myself but my love for stability does not mean that I cannot handle change. In times past, I am talking about 20-25 years ago, business owners were used to comfort and less unpredictable change in business. Today, the world is a global village and the era of instant communication with people all over the four corners of the earth have caused the era of comfort to end. These days, business owners have learnt to stay on their toes and constantly look out for changes that may occur in order to avoid shocking surprises.

This factor coupled with others has presented most senior executives with an unfamiliar challenge. Today, large enterprises and their advisors focus their attention on devising the best strategic and tactical plans that will handle whatever new development(s) they may face. In order to succeed I today's ever-dynamic world of business, business owners must have an intimate understanding of the human side of change management. What is this human side? It deals with the alignment of the company's culture, values, people, and behaviors in order to encourage the desired results. Plans themselves do not capture value; value can only be realized through the continuous and collective actions of employees who are responsible for designing, executing, and living with the changed environment. In the business world, once you are able to handle the human aspect of the response to change, then you have done the most part of the task.

Long-term structural transformation has to go through four characteristic stages:

- Firstly the scale of such change, it tends to affect a larger and more significant aspect of the organization
- Secondly the weight of such change, this might involve severe changes being made to the status quo

- Thirdly, the time frame of such changes, typically such changes are bound to last for months or even years depending on the size of such a business.

- Lastly, this kind of change will lead to a change in the strategy of the company involved and might take a while before it gets to each employee of such a company. This stage is also largely determined by the size of the company involved.

Adjusting to change

For most senior executives, the problem with change rests in the fact that adapting to it will take a lot of time and effort before it gets to individual employees. Also, it is going to take a lot of effort to convince each individual to accept that change. If you happen to lead a relatively large set of people and you are considering how difficult it will be to effect the change that you have always wanted to effect, here are some tips that you might find helpful in your bid to properly manage change;

- Pay attention to the human side of effecting change because it is the most important and ensure that it is done systematically.
- It is best to begin at the Apex of the organization because those are the people that others look to for motivation, strength and direction

- Do not miss any layer in the process of transformation, as you begin from the apex you should ensure that you go down step by step in the company's chain of command. The various leaders at various levels should be saddled with the responsibility of implementing such change to those that are directly under them.

- Stating that you want to change is not enough; you should clearly state why you think the change is in line with the company's vision. By doing this, you are ensuring that everyone who believed in the company's vision haven't stopped believing and this belief will cause them to work even harder and make the change process even easier.

- If you desire change then you should show that you desire it by being the motivator and others will definitely follow in your steps. If you are able to lead by example and show zeal and appetite for success, then the process of change will be easier and more fun for everyone on the team. If members of your company that look up to you are able to see the zeal and hunger for success in you then they will commit to the process whole-heartedly.

- It is wrong to assume that the people under you will have a clear understanding of the issues that necessitated change in the first place. As a leader, it is important for you to clearly and constantly pass across the message of change to the people under you because they need to hear it from YOU.

- Before deciding to embark on a change mission, ensure to consider the conditions that will be as a result of such a change and check if they align with the core values of your company. You do not want to be seen as a confused leader with contradictory ideals.

- If you expect the unexpected then it becomes the expected; it is very likely that the change program that you are embarking on will not totally go according to plan therefore it is very important that you plan for certain pitfalls that might happen along the line.

- For a lot of people, their work is a very vital part of their lives therefore it is very important to relay the idea of change and how it will make their work life better to them on a personal note. This might not be possible for very large companies but as much as possible, try to create a personal feeling of involvement for every employee. This can be done by sending personalized emails (in the case of large businesses); if you are able to make the change process seem like a personal journey then members of your team will definitely put their best efforts into making the change effective as quickly as possible.

CHAPTER EIGHT: IMPORTANCE OF BRAND POSITIONING

As the name implies, brand positioning is the process of using a particular strategy or a set of strategies in ensuring that your brand holds a particular position in the mind of your customers. What comes to mind of a customer when your brand name is mentioned? What do your customers (and non-customers) recognize your brand for? I love using the example of a brand like Apple Inc. What do you think of when you hear that brand name? You will probably hear something along the lines of luxury and quality. Overtime this brand has been positioned in such a way that their products have become more or less like a kind of lifestyle choice. This is why brand positioning is very essential, if done properly it can help your business immensely as it will help you to stay in the minds of people once they hear the name of your brand. Various strategies including promotions, marketing, packaging, pricing among others can be used in the process of positioning a brand. The end goal of positioning is to create a certain unique impression on the mind of the customer so that he/she associates a distinct feature to your brand.

Sometimes brand positioning is overlooked as being unimportant but that is not in any way correct because the position of a brand helps brands to differentiate themselves. If you are in a crowded industry and you need to be recognized differently because of the product or service you offer, you are going to have to do more than mentioning how different your brand it. Typically, every brand claims to be the best at what they do; therefore, customers need more than just assurance. More-so, there is a high chance that there are several other competitors that offer the same service or make the same product therefore you need to find a proper position for your brand that will set you apart from the rest. Permit me to tell you that the positioning of your brand is somewhat similar to its unique selling point. Positioning is the process of properly identifying a need, problem or opportunity and developing a well-sought out solution based on information gotten from the customers through market research and other necessary data. The issue of positioning can be summarized in the answer to one question, what reason(s) will convince a customer to buy your product or service from time to time instead of the countless alternatives? Positioning is not what you do to a product rather positioning is what you do to the mind of the prospective buyer. Simply put, it is the way you position the product in the mind of the prospect, the idea of the sort of satisfaction that will be derived from purchasing your product or your services. If done properly, the customer will have maximum trust in your product and this will cause him/her to always seek to use your products or pay for your services. Any other brand will seem below par.

The idea of having your brand properly positioned in the mind of the consumer is lovely right? Now let us look at the process of positioning your brand in the mind of the consumer. You will need to identify your brand's USP, as it is what differentiates you from your competitors. If you do not have a Unique Selling Point then you need to look for it and in the process of looking for it is important to make realistic promises because creating a standard in the mind of the consumer and not living up to that standard could cost your company a lot. Below are steps that you should take in order to correctly determine your position in the marketplace;

- Take out time to identify your brand's current position in the market.
- Identify your direct competitors and how they have positioned their brand.
- Compare your brand's positioning to that of your competitors

- Develop your brand's unique and value-based positioning idea.

There are certain important elements and questions to consider when positioning your brand and in doing this you will need to create a brand positioning statement that will spell out the true position that you want your brand to occupy in the mind of the consumers.

1) Who are your target customers? In positioning your brand, you need to know the kind of minds in which you want your brand to be positioned. What is the age group of your target customers? What social class do you want them to

be from? What group of people do you want your brand to appeal to?

2) Also you need to clearly define the market that you are operating in and the context in which your brand will be relevant to consumers

3) Thirdly, you need to create a promise (that your brand will clearly fulfill) that will appeal to the emotional part of your customer. This aspect is important because more often than not, purchases are influenced by emotional factors more than financial , rational and other forms of influence

4) Lastly, your brand promises cannot be just ordinary promises, as they must be backed up with real evidence of your brand's ability to fulfill its promises to its customers.

If you are able to create a great brand positioning statement and then match it with a magnificent product or service that matches the promises made in the statement then you will enjoy the loyalty of your customers as long as your product is made with the same quality every single time.

CHAPTER NINE: ATTACKING BY FIRE

The great warrior Sun Tzu said: "There are five ways of attacking with fire. The first is to burn soldiers in their camp; the second is to burn stores; the third is to burn baggage trains; the fourth is to burn arsenals and magazines; the fifth is to hurl dropping fire amongst the enemy".

Every time you decide to launch an attack on your enemies, you should be sure that you have the right resources to launch the attack and also you must be certain that you are doing it at the right season. The timing of an attack can be the difference between victory and defeat. Also, in order to successfully carry out an attack you must have the means to carry out the attack and then see to it that you successfully defeat the enemy. If you are not certain about your ability to successfully launch a proper attack then you should not bother attacking in the first place. There is an added advantage if you can attack your enemy with an element of surprise; the best time to launch an attack is when the enemy least expects it. In attacking by 'fire' you should always endeavor to keep the materials for raising fire ready.

Seasons are also very important to consider when you are planning on launching an attack with fire. There are times when fire will readily burn and there are other seasons when the fire will hardly burn. If you launch an attack with fire during those kinds of seasons like winter, you might just end up losing such a battle. Similarly, in the business world it is important to put timing into critical consideration before launching an attack. Attacking by fire connotes that you are going all out against your enemy, therefore if you do not properly plan such an attack and it fails, the counter attack from such an enemy could be very disastrous. Take out your time and understand the aspect of your competitor's business that you intend to attack. Real time warriors spend more time on the drawing board because that is where battles are won. The proper season to launch an attack by fire is when the weather is very dry because that is when "nature's fuel" will support your attack.

Attacking the competitor is just one step, what do you do after launching the attack? Keep in mind that your enemy will respond to the attack, the level to which this attack will affect you will depend largely on the next steps that you take. After launching, the first attack and you see the signs of trouble in the camp of your enemies then you should go to the next line of attack, if you are able to cause chaos in your enemy's camp then you can strike with another attack from outside that danger zone. There is an exception to this principle though; if you attack your enemy by fire and the enemy doesn't respond then you should not attack immediately. There are times when plans of your attack will leak to the enemy and they will prepare for it, in that kind of scenario you cannot afford to continue to attack because it might eventually backfire. This is why it is very important to keep plans of your attack as a secret that only top ranking people on your team know about. If you have generals that you cannot trust on your team then you will probably never know victory, therefore it is important to check your closest allies to be sure that there are no loopholes.

After launching the first attack, find a favorable moment where your competitor is vulnerable and launch further attacks to compound your enemy's woes. I have emphasized patience in different parts of this book and here it is also needed; patience and vigilance are necessary when you are attacking by fire because you will need to launch further attacks at the perfect time to ensure victory.

Timing is also an important factor, do you launch your attack during the daytime (when it is visible for all to see) or do you have the resources to launch the attack at night? What comes next after you must have successfully launched the attack? You should have a clearly established plan that will guide you every step of the way; you do not launch an attack and then begin to wonder what to do next. You must have a strategy ready for every point of attack because if you give the enemy time, such an enemy could gather the spoils and then launch a reprisal attack. You do not want to give your competitor the benefit of having the time to gather spoils therefore your attack should be an all-out attack.

Attacking by fire is not something that warriors do at the slightest provocation; it is not a battle that is fought to defend a general's pride or some other selfish agenda. Attacking by fire is mostly a last resort and it is meant for your archrival because not only does it take a lot of planning but because it could put you in danger if it isn't done properly. As a leader, you cannot afford to let anger get the better of you, your reason for war (especially by fire) should never be personal because anger can change to gladness in no time. If you decide to go all out in war then it should be for a cause that is worth fighting for. As I stated earlier in the book, as a leader you should try to win most battles without actually fighting. If however, you have seen the need, you have the right resources to attack by fire and you have the perfect strategy then by all means you should attack by fire!

CONCLUSION: THE DAY AFTER-REMAINING ON TOP

Today, the world is in a way that only the strongest will survive; you have to be willing to fight and conquer boundaries in order to get to the top and stay there. The road to the top is narrow and not everyone will be willing to do what it takes to be there, therefore, you have to ask yourself if you are willing to do what it takes to get to the top and stay there. You have to be willing to fight, you have to be willing to conquer; you must be willing to take territories because that is the way to the top. It is never a personal war; it is a necessary war that must be fought in order to separate the feeble minded from the greats. War is the earth's way of distributing resources and in life you do not get what you deserve, you only get what you are willing to fight for. Are you willing to go to war for what you love? Are you willing to fight for the lifestyle that you desire? Are you willing to fight to remain at the top?

The climb to the top is a really hectic one that requires a lot of patience, hard work, resilience, team building, risk taking, failure, perseverance and a host of other things. One fact is that if you can decide on a goal for yourself and stay hungry then you will get there, it is only a matter of time. Getting to the top is the easier aspect of greatness, staying on top can prove to be really tough and here's why: When you are climbing to the top, people do not know who you are and those who do are not bothered by you because you do not pose as a threat to them.

Once you are able to gain grounds in whatever niche you have chosen to focus on, you will be faced with opposition from all angles; people will try to break you down (not because they hate you) but because they want what you have. You do not get to the top and then decide to relax because that will definitely be suicidal, there is no new secret regarding how you can maintain your position at the top; it is the same thing that you did when you were climbing that you need to continually do in order to stay on top.

The reason why most people fall is that while they are climbing, they stay hungry and eager for success but get distracted when they get up there. This should not be you, getting to the top is something worth celebrating but you should not get lost in the glamour that comes with being on top. Also, it is important that you network and have allies that will support you because no man is an island of knowledge on his own, therefore, you will need to have friends at every level of the way.

Failure. I love failure! Yes I said that. Most times, people love to live in the illusion that failure is avoidable but the truth is that it is a road bump on the way to success. You must never be afraid to fail because the man who has never failed is the man who has never tried something new. Failure teaches you a lot, it teaches you attitude, it teaches you perseverance, and it teaches you to believe in yourself, it teaches you to take risks amongst other lessons. Therefore, if you are to be scared of anything, then it should not be failure because it is inevitable.

Believe, for it is said that a man that believes in himself is an unstoppable man. Do not stop believing in yourself, humans are capable of anything only if we can put our minds to it. Take a look at most of the billionaires that we have in the world today, many of them were not raised by billionaires, a handful them were raised by ordinary middle class or even lower class citizens but through the believe they had in themselves and in their dream, they climbed to the apex by constantly warring. Do not stop believing in yourself, the problem with humans is that we get distracted by the things happening around us and these distractions hinder us from getting to our goals. Be focused, be hungry, and be willing to learn, be willing to grow, be willing to try, and be willing to fail because the only harm is when you are not willing to try.

Time is of the essence as it is the only thing that we all have in equal proportion as humans. What you choose to do with your time matters a lot, do not live life with the illusion that you have a lot of time; do what you need to do today because that is the only time that you are promised. Tomorrow is a prospect that never really comes; all we do is look forward to it with hope and faith for the best. Timing is also very important, the Christian holy book talks about how there is a time for everything: a time to sow, a time to reap, a time to live and a time to die. Time is of the essence and timing can change a lot.

Finally, I want to tell you that if you have come this far on this journey with me, then I expect to see you at the top. I believe that you are capable of whatever you put your mind to, it is never too late to start anything, if you think so then read up on the story of the founder of KFC. You are never too young to start anything, if you think so read up on the story of the founder of Facebook. People will tell you things about yourself and it is up to you to believe it or not. You are the captain of your own ship, you are the master of your fate, you can make a difference and you will if you decide to put your heart to it. Successful people are just everyday people who decided to make something out of their lives, all you need is to make that decision and stick with it. If anyone is an opposition on your way to success then I urge you to declare war on them today!